cooling board
a long-playing poem

Mitchell L. H. Douglas

cooling board

a long-playing poem

Mitchell L. H. Douglas

RED HEN PRESS | LOS ANGELES, CALIFORNIA

Engineered by Mark E. Cull, assisted by Sydney Nichols
Cover artwork: "Mr. Hathaway: The Remix" by Krista Franklin

ISBN: 978-1-59709-140-4
Library of Congress Catalog Card Number: 2008942402

The California Arts Council and the National Endowment for the Arts partially support Red Hen Press.

Produced by Red Hen Press
www.redhen.org
First Edition

For Nicole, Little Mitchell & Nia. My family, my heart.

ACKNOWLEDGEMENTS

Grateful acknowledgement is made to the editors of the following publications in which these poems first appeared or are forthcoming:

"On Country & Western" is forthcoming in *Ninth Letter*; "Essex House Hotel" and "Roberta, Rebirth" appeared in *Zoland Poetry*, Volume II, Zoland Books, 2008; "The Music: An Explanation to Miss Martha" appeared in *The Louisville Review*, Fall 2006; "Notes On 'Life,' a Symphony" is a found poem based on an interview with Donny Hathaway by WBLS radio, New York, New York; "Diagnosis, 1973" is a found poem based on information available at www.mayoclinic.com.

SPECIAL THANKS: to the Affrilachian Poets / Frank X Walker (for always putting me in the right place at the right time) / Cave Canem and the faculty of 2007: Toi Derricotte, Cornelius Eady, Patricia Smith, Erica Hunt (your contacts helped complete this book), Cyrus Cassells, Yusef Komunyakaa, and Carl Phillips / Jacqueline Bethany / J.D. Parran / Charles Wartts / Alfred Netterville / Angela Borders / the Indiana University-Purdue University Indianapolis School of Liberal Arts / Kevin Young (the long poem class was a revelation) / DeLana Dameron / Krista Franklin / Mom & Dad (always) / and the city of St. Louis.

Playlist

SIDE TWO

Hang on to the world
as it spins around,
just don't let the spin
get you down—

        —Donny Hathaway,
          "Someday We'll All Be Free"

cooling board

a long-playing poem

Like any project by Donny Hathaway, the social and spiritual conscious of '70s and '80s R&B, *Cooling Board* is cause for celebration. This posthumous collection of studio rarities and unreleased live performances finds the legendary singer/composer at a crossroads: contemplating the success of his partnership with Roberta Flack ("The Last Supper: Roberta's Apartment, Central Park West"); the guidance of his grandmother, Martha Crumwell ("The Music: An Explanation to Miss Martha"); and his future as an artist who saw beyond the boundaries of conventional soul ("Notes on 'Life,' a Symphony"). *Cooling Board* is about life lessons, the difficult things you don't always get on the first take. With each endeavor, Hathaway proves such trials are worth the struggle. In an age of reality-TV-assembled throwaway artists, *Cooling Board* is a musical throwback: a long-playing album meant for one long, contemplative listen. What we, Hathaway's faithful, are left with is another testament to his greatness and the overwhelming sense of his absence. Listen, be reminded and renewed.

cooling board
a long-playing poem
Mitchell L. H. Douglas
Side One

side
ONE
· · · · · · · · · ·

Essex House Hotel

Had a hard time trying
to break that pane without someone
running to my door, questioning
the commotion. Picked a corner, tapped

with a pocket knife, my Bible's spine. The glass
thin-ice cracked, shifted, left spaces
to the other side. Wound a tear of sheet
'round my fingers, pressed soft against sharp,

head turned to snap the clear—
each piece for the pile
a lens on a cloudless Manhattan,
sapphire cape draping steel shoulders.

A ladder   rungless   waiting.

NAMING

Why heap the weight
of a man you don't know
on your back, sentence
you to drag his load
all your days?

I won't be the one.

How can I justify
the wrap of an absent hand
'round your neck,
brand you with the cost
of your father?

& why can't I
give you the steel of my spine—
Hathaway, not Brown—
rock you to sleep
with the root of my father?

This I promise,
God as my witness,
winged confidant.
He is no stranger
to my pain.

Exodus I (Chicago to St. Louis)

for Drusella Huntley

Sure as the rags on your back
are my woven arms, I will
wrap you, tighter,
against the wind,
until there is no skin
for a breeze
to crack.

    There will be words:
how I turned my eyes south,
my back to Chicago,
how the lake, great
wishing well, don't wave
like it used to. All those fingers
wag, but they know:
raising a boy alone in a city of wind
is a lesson
no woman wants.

    Never mind frail:
    Miss Martha's legs are fragile,

but none can fault her heart.
So we'll raise a roof together
where the streets know more
about sun, love you
like Chicago was never cold
& nothing ever crests, breaks
in a gust of dawn.

Ascension (A Lesson for Miss Martha)

Church.   Church & God.
I don't know how else
to say it.

      Every Sunday
Donny hears me rise early,
start the biscuits & bacon,

practice the solo
just in case Sister Wilson
don't show.

      Every service,
Donny takes notes with his eyes,
spies my gestures to stretch soprano,

let baritone roll low. After church, I push
a microphone toward the floor,
hang a ukulele on his shoulder,

rest the tiny body on his belly.
Play what the Lord put on your heart,
I say, *here's your ticket.*

He looks through the roof,
past me, eyes
all china & coffee.

Three years old
& ten times wise,
his fingers

mark the strings
like dog-eared pages
in my favorite hymnal,

dance like a scroll
unfurled, the scripture
most revered.

The Amazing Donny Pitts & His Magic Ukulele

Look at him—look at the way
he rocks so far over, left

to right, like some invisible hand
keeps him from tipping,

never wishing Donny lost.
          He can play that ukulele

like he made that ukulele,
tap a foot to keep time,

fingers that never tire, just strum
& slide, strum & slide.

          When's the last time
you seen something like that?

So beautiful, your head
tells your lips what to say

& they still can't get it right.
Night after night,

folks ask his age, tell me
I'm lying when I reply

he's only been 'round long enough
to see December

salt the ground three times.
That's three times plenty.

THE MUSIC: AN EXPLANATION TO MISS MARTHA

Birds are the first thing
like the morning,

a smiling rising call—that's my horn section.
The way pop bottles clink, even break, & jump ropes

 slap concrete when the pretty girls double-dutch.
That's my rhythm.

There's the grate of the screen door—
open, close—how water in your kettle

rustles over fire, that sound
just shy of a whistle— my guitars, violins.

I wrote it for you, Grandma, a Sunday song
to swing the choir's robes, make the church

say "Amen" he says. All I hear is "Chopsticks,"
"Three Blind Mice," but the way he looks at me,

his eyes on my eyes, fixed, never falling,
the way the future unfurls, his fingers

still planted on the keys,
I can't help but believe.

EXTENSIONS

Soon as I give Donny that ukulele,
set him loose on revivals, Sunday socials,
he ditched it for a piano,

said that little guitar didn't work
for the music in his head.
He stopped working that finger

& thumb, sat down at my piano
a good long time,
not touching, just thinking

what would happen
if this finger went here, there.
They say if you know one

you can figure the other—
guitar & piano that is.

Children ain't that simple.

TRYING TIMES, CENTRAL CITY

Our names are written in stone,
spray can nozzles spit
these daily psalms.

      Our street lamps moonlight
as stars. Have you ever seen
where I come from?

      Each sunrise bathes me
in hi-hat smiles, bass drum
hearts. Kind souls with flat pockets

offer what they can, say
Here baby— for you
& Miss Martha.

All this warm can erase
rust, bricks more at home
at our feet than raising walls.

There's talk of building
an arch, sway of steel so high
fools'll think they can walk

to heaven. Round here
we know better. Figure
someday, that arch

would turn too, flake & fall
like every block
in my brick city.

Moving Days

Who can match our pace?
Childhood of infinite numbers,

new streets = new strangers.
Hard to welcome another start

when I thought last time
was the last time.

      I've seen Biddle Street,
North Maffit, Carr Lane,

Cole. O'Fallon Elementary,
Simmons Elementary, Wheatley—

more.
      What we own

fits in pockets, wraps
shoulders calm. Live

this lesson early:
Anywhere's a long walk home.

ANATOMY

Call it a great wood wing,
ebony sail for a vessel
anchored in pine. Its curve
can pass for a spine:

dip of dark
an invitation
to hammered timbre, a sound
that can't be bartered.

Music is always, Grandma said
when she parted my scalp, hot
with the tug of her heavy hand.
Cool blue pomade quelled the fire

until the next pull, the next match
strike of the steel-toothed rake,
her seasoned fingers.
Call it irrigation. Grandma cut paths

in fields of black cotton, giving back a love
like the piano, black well of sound,
its night & day fingers
anticipating the reach of mine.

Tell me that's not my body
in tone & touch,
that both of us
don't break, bleed.

Midnight Hour

He plays when dreams come, when
the hour is as late as the moon
allows, when
ribbons of light
slice window panes, shine
for the sake of sight.
       Can you play
your fingers ivory,
no difference between keys
& bones? Can you lean
into the first note
like the strain
to catch a faint voice, everything
sweet whispered
worth something?
        Sometimes,
I raise the blanket
over my head,
try to pretend I don't hear
him reach for notes

that aren't there. Without
the sight, we know the sound:
a key pressed again & again
like a voice cracking, the pause,
the echo of ten fingers
walking the plank
of shadow & light.

The hidden.
The longing.

Donny Hathaway playing with his
grandmother, Martha Crumwell.
From private family photo collection.
Courtesy of Jacqueline Bethany.

Exodus II (St. Louis to D.C.)

My future is on a black campus
in a black city, capital
of a nation Nam wired,
Nixon weary.

     When I leave St. Louis,
Grandma is already at the market,
cleaning catfish for early risers, saving
a taste for herself.

     Do right boy, is how she leaves me,
before a day's salt & scale
flood her knotted fingers. At home,
she will rinse the grind from her hands

     remember her orders
to me each evening on how to scrub
the sink as she inches away, eyes
on a bath spiked with Epsom.

Circles, baby.   *In circles.*

Meeting Eulaulah, Howard University

I heard her sing—

notes as wings, butterfly or bird, the sound
of flowers if we could hear
the petals' work—

& in my head, I'm on a bus
to St. Louis, wondering what Grandma
will think of my Eulaulah.

        Open your mouth,
Eulaulah says, *let your own notes spill,*
but I am pleased with the piano:

the give of the bench, the keys'
gap-toothed smile, a gospel
that sings me whole.

…& she thinks my voice

could rouse a crowd, ring
above this song?

•

WHAT EULAULAH HEARS

Singing is out, he says—
like raised voices
are meant to be discarded,
discovered years later

like outgrown clothes
in attics of dust.
I have never met someone
so blessed yet so afraid

to share the gifts
God gave.
       Not the keys,
he gives that freely, the proof

of so many Sundays, rocking
the choir holy.
       It is written in him,
by & by, words

too bright for a back to turn.
I can pray all day, but that boy is crazy
if he doesn't let the world
hear him sing.

I loved his song
before I knew his name.

Negotiating the First Date

Afternoon,
        evening
Revival,
        movie
Staple Singers,
           Sam Cooke
Fried chicken,
        chicken salad

Walk in the park
        park, don't walk—

if I had a ride. Maybe we can start
with your hand, mine.

WHAT STARS ARE FOR

My hand is an anchor
linked to each slip of her finger,
a weight at her side, the heft

to keep her here. I grip tighter,
gathering the links, no slack,
no room to run.

Back at Vashon, a boy
passed a note to a girl
named Sister, asked her

"Do you like me? Check yes
or no"— she left the boxes
blank. & Loretta, the senior

he invited for Cokes at Walgreens, said yes,
never showed, told her friends
who never tired of a point & taunt.

Eulaulah smiles, eases my grip,
points to the North Star
with her free hand. And I'm sure

when stars flicker
like a mass of staring eyes
stopped to blink, the moon

so happily gorged,
there are wishes at work:

those just granted,
others waiting turn.

Meeting Eulaulah, Howard University (alternate take)

Picture me, compelled
to ditch class over you,
the question

Prof. Burge's contralto
can't account for:
What happens when a voice

makes you fall?
Not forgotten alto
on a scratched 45,

but 5 feet of pink sweater,
plaid skirt, singing
like freshman chorus was her invention.

A sparrow at the window, I stare
even when she catches
my eyes.

Roberta, Rebirth

You're all this campus can talk about

Donny says, our hands
a fallen metronome. I speak
of spirituals, "Come Ye Disconsolate,"

what my mother sings
when her heart is light.
        If your Missouri

is anything like my Carolinas,
you have your own Black Mountains.
Corner or forest, they know

strife, stand strong above the plain.
        We roll out of those hills
with a song on our tongues,

share music of cascading rock,
fir needles on the wind—
the difference

between whine & wail.

MISS MARTHA MEETS EULAULAH

When Donny walked her through my front door,
I held my tongue. What kind of name is Eulaulah

anyhow? She smiled, extended her hand, skin
too soft for work. They sipped iced tea

like humming birds on honeysuckle, made goo goo eyes,
thought I couldn't see. Donny took her hand,

led her to my piano & played
"It Is Well With My Soul."   Then she sang.

That girl's all right with me.

ROBERTA, REBIRTH (ALTERNATE TAKE)

I swear that hat is halo:
Horizon for a brim, cloud

of wool with a star
for a button top. It's his eyes

that get you, what you can see
under the dip of the cap.

They say, *I know you sister.*
You're all this campus can talk about.

When he extends his hand,
there is nothing left to do

but smile
& reach.

Curtis Breaks It Down

Doo Wop schooled us
on a South Side corner, pitching
wolf howls at the moon. Me
and my other-mother-brothers,
all we had was a dream.
                              Not gonna say
your spoon was silver, but your life
is charmed: my singing never got me
a scholarship or shipped off
to a fancy school just for us.
But my music has taken me places,
can't deny that, & we both
felt the spirit move us from the pew
to the truth. Look brother,
it's all Chicago. I see it in you.

We want, we hustle.

TRIO

Hole in the wall
is a compliment, play

on a trip of carpet,
plywood, drift. Piano

sideways so the crowd can see
me work, Ric on backbeat,

Phil's bass: our steady, heavy rock.
Brothers laugh at me for being green,

tightening my face
as cigarette trails slap cheeks.

But the money is good, better
than Grandma's fish market change,

reason to miss class,
keep the joint jumping 'til morning:

every body fluid,
every glass filled.

S.R.O.: Mr. Henry's, Capitol Hill

       Got a space for me upstairs:
pews & an upright
just like daddy's church
with a little more shouting,
a lot less religion.
       I can save Donny
a seat in the front
where the suits & ties
come in off the Hill, rest their bones
in a bourbon soak.
       The second show
is always more crowded,
like word got around
the girl upstairs is teasing demons
out the piano.
       Standing in the center makes you dizzy,
the way the waitress takes orders, turns
sharp, the glasses—sweating
halos—lined up
like sinners for sermon.

I steady myself at the keys,
hear the creak of the bench,
call on a song
carved in the road
of my palm.

Troubadour, 1971

California sisters don't sit back,
they sing back—sip gin & tonics,
slap a girlfriend's shoulder,

shout "Go 'head"
& "That's all right"
from the tables

by the exit.
                    We are music:
You, backup without microphones,

stand-ins for Roberta on "You Got a Friend";
me, a midnight declaration
through the heat of red lights,

electric keys.
                    Sing,
sing with me

California sisters,
like the marquee bears your name,
& the man who wouldn't spring for a ticket

can hear you carry on
from the couch at home. Sing,
like the bartender's last call

is the last call you'll ever hear,
& you can't leave
until you hit every note just so.

     Sing,
sing with me
California sisters,

over brick thick cigarette smog,
the off-beat clap
of Mr.One-Whisky-Too-Many, the hip

slap & shake of a crescent tambourine
rattling like a gourd of cowrie shells,
Angel City cat call, ancient bell.

Earl summons a conga pop
with the cup of his hands,
Phil picks & skips, teases

a tip-toe rhythm
low E to high.
Willie pulls those four strings

into a trance that thumps
through our chests
& the scream starts in the front row

hits the back wall
& Marshall reverb hums
over our bowed heads—

each & every hand caught
in a soul clap, inseparable song:
no instrument greater

than the next.
        Sing,
sing with me

California sisters.
This is no place to live
unheard.

The Bitter End

No alcohol served,
not a note from the crowd.

Tonight, the spotlight
is lonely.

cooling board
a long playing poem

Mitchell L. H. Douglas
Side Two

side
TWO
· · · · · · · · ·

Notes on 'Life,' a Symphony

Composed: Jan. 1, 1972

Movements:

The good,
the bad,

the positive,
the negative,

the dull,
the tension,

the calm.

cooling board

a long-playing poem

Your ears will burn. There will be no differentiation between sight and sound. This is the magic of Donny Hathaway. A legend in the making, Hathaway is an incomparable musician who has earned the respect of his peers and the public alike. Hathaway strikes gold again with his latest release *Cooling Board*. Please buy into the idea that music is transformative, that you will somehow be forever changed when the needle drops and the first notes fill the room. We, the record company, can't guarantee this, but we do, without the artist's knowledge, however we can.

Sure, it's a lot like lying on a resume, but everyone lies on resumes. What would it sound like if we said "Sorry, we goofed. Donny had a bunch of unreleased tracks we knew nothing about until a recording engineer stumbled across them one day and said, "Take a look at this." We'd like to say your world will change, and I'm sure Donny would like to make it happen. He's that kind of guy. The reality is you gave this a shot. You spent your cash, now you want some-thing in return. You want the proof.

THE HIP

is not a matter
of what's in or out,

cool or cold,
but the marvelous curve

that resides between your stomach & thigh,
calls me when your lips don't move,

thrusts left, hoists
our seeds to air, rests

the mesh of you & me
on its precious axis.

JINGLES

Soul can sell cigarettes, cancer
& burn, sell two all beef patties,
special-sauce-lettuce-cheese, the green
grease that lines your scalp,
makes your cornrows gleam,
turn Afros
into earth-bound satellites.
      Soul can sell suburbia:
do-gooder white family
with sassy black maid
named after a state
where Africans & Indians
turned brothers, understood
the insanity of serving anyone
who claims to own
your blood.
      Soul can sell soul,
can sell your soul—the only soul
you've known. With a wife,
two babies, soul will be sold

if the money's right
& our bellies don't have to growl
tonight.

The Uninvited (Visitor 1)

It's all right. You didn't expect her
to understand, did you? I'm talking

about Eulaulah. Look man,
all you got to do is think

about you. What I mean is,
how many ladies really understand

an artist? Okay, she's an artist too,
but two artists married, raising babies—

that's disaster. Especially since your art
is her art. She's not a partner,

she's competiton. Better jump ship
before she gets tired, fires

you first. Hear me,
Donny? Donny, can you hear me?

'Course you can. Nothing's wrong
with your ears.

Sessions: New York

What the people want are Siamese twins
joined at the throat, two-headed
song bird regurgitating hits:
robots, Roberta & Donny.

How many ways
can we give the world
Roberta & Donny
Donny & Roberta

Roberta featuring Donny
Roberta.
Roberta.
Roberta.

Stop me
if you've heard this one before.

WHISPERERS

My ghosts don't wait for dark.

My ears are their homes,
murmurs in the nooks

behind the drums. Nothing
I can say they can't tell first,

braggarts of sorts, quick with the tongue.
My lips splice the air in answers,

But for whom? Eulaulah asks.
    For whom?

     Just the thought,
& my lips are listless,
my only offer
a drape of air   still.

An Evening at St. Vincent

Eulaulah calls it salve, says
You'll feel better here,

but salve is a sweet way of saying
Down this bitter pill:

a white room, the burn
of some steely antiseptic,

lost access to your assets,
replacements of throwaway gowns,

the gap & tie at your back.
No belts.   No laces.

If this is salve, give me the ghosts,
the torch of their whispers.

At least I know
they lie.

Diagnosis, 1973

There's often no cure
for the illness, but by working closely

with a psychologist & other mental
health professionals, schizophrenia

can be managed successfully—especially
with an early diagnosis. Fortunately,

newer medications continue
to make this poorly understood

order more
manageable.

Meds

Count them out, give each one
a day. Don't care

what you call it—this is
an awkward dance.

Feels like something other
than. Tell you

I'm better,

but here you are: scarecrow
in the doorway,

two promises
in your palm,

a stare that says
swallow.

This Is Blues

You have grown tired of subtlety,
so the same bag I took to Howard,
stuffed a few pairs of slacks

& my good sweaters in,
is packed, waiting at the door.
Your heart knows it's 2 a.m., knows

you could've changed your mind.
But when you packed the bag
that evening at 6, you say, you never

took anything out, just kept adding
the forgotten, hoping
there was room.

In Case You Thought It Was Easy

Our first date, that soul food place
near campus, you
feeding me corn pudding

with a crooked spoon, your hand
beneath my chin
to catch what my lips could not.

The day you gave a single rose,
said one is for love,
one dozen for show.

The look on your face
when I sing,
like you want to know the notes,

be where they come from.
That perfume you bought
'cause you thought it was my favorite,

forgot it was the one I said I'd never wear,
whatever pigs grew wings or fires froze.
(I wore it every blessed day

'til the bottle ran dry).
Our daughters asking why
daddy can't come home.

Should I go on?

THE UNINVITED (VISITOR 2)

Use the spine God gave you, & you wouldn't have to deal with half the mess you complain about daily, Donny. Think I'm not listening? If I can't hear, why is every note the same? Can't figure out how you got this way. Do you look like wallpaper? They don't know you Donny Hathaway? You the voice people want, & you doing more than singing. Composing, arranging—everything. Donny Hathaway. What's that name gonna mean if you don't stand up & scream? You wanna be loved like Ray, like Otis, like Stevie (don't forget Marvin)? Donny…Dahnaay! Don't play like you can't hear me. I'll bare my head, dare you to speak my name.

CHART POSITION (WHAT HITS & WHAT DOES NOT, TAKE 1)

"I Thank You Baby" (w/June Conquest) 1969 (First single, fails to chart)

"The Ghetto" 1970 (First solo single, R&B #23)

"I Love You More Than You'll Ever Know" 1972 (R&B #20)

"You've Got a Friend" (w/Roberta Flack) 1972 (R&B Top 10)

"Love, Love, Love" 1973 (R&B #16)

Release Me

Tell her,
> This is how it's gotta be,
don't be afraid—
> I am somebody without you.
The timing
> I know that now,
couldn't be better.
> Each time, I think
You know everything,
> it will be different
don't fool yourself
> it never is. I just keep hoping,
you notice the need.
> singing out of windows,
This is our secret
> waiting for the wind to take my voice
don't tell a soul.
> somewhere better.

Phantom Limb

How, after
the note is released
does the body remember
the hunger?

　　　Does the foot rise
& dive, do the hands
hammer? In the inner ear,
what echo comes once,

makes a home?
My heart's drumming
is a solitary song, the rifle
of stick & skin. One hand

bound, the other
in spite of.

(Re)union

Daddy, I have grown
without you, lived
a life worth knowing, choosing
humility over holler, the Lord
leading my heart's ears.

Somebody took your place.

Granddaddy was a railroad man,
sped out of St. Louis further
into riot & flame, made enough food
appear on the table for Momma, Grandma,
Jackie, & me. Are you
that kind of man, Daddy? The kind
that conjures sacrifice, shows little concern
for self?

Come. Take your place.

Daddy, I have grown
in spite of you, lived
a life without chase, knowing
there is no grace
without humility, no holler
that can be heard
above the Lord.

You could say I'm no stranger
to slight of hand. Each day in lack
I consider our trials, siphon
our blessings.

On Country & Western

I dig the simplicity:
white blues with banjos, boxcars
from the rails of our burden.

Everybody's got something
to ache for: love, or lack of,
what we want & will never

be privileged to. I heard Johnny Cash
talk about doing shows
behind bars. Folsom, San Quentin,

how all those men living caged
might rest a little easier
hearing him, feel a day or two

slip off a 20-year bid. I wonder
if there's room for lap steel
in rhythm & blues,

harmonica like Hank
instead of Stevie?
If I sang country,

would America buy a black man
out of costume—pick fiddles
over saxophones, spurs

for walking shoes?
What bars would break,
souls heal?

This Is Blues (alternate take)

At 2 a.m., I wanted to know
where we stood on the fight
that made me leave that afternoon—

your answer, my suitcase packed,
stationed at the door. Subtlety has no place
with you, wore off when the studio uptown

became my bedroom. The suitcase isn't phased,
still as shabby as the day I left St. Louis,
stuffed it with slacks, my good sweaters.

Your heart knows its 2 a.m., knows
you could've changed your mind,
but when the bag was packed at 6,

you say, nothing ever came out,
& you called a dozen hotels
for a vacant room.

Roberta, Rebirth (alternate take 2)

You're all this campus can talk about,

Donny says, the difference between whine
& wail. Our hands, fir needles

on the wind, a fallen metronome.
I speak of spirituals, share music

of cascading rock—what my mother sings—
with a song on our tongues. When her heart is light,

we roll out of those hills. If your Missouri
strife stands strong above the plain

anything like my Carolinas, corner
or forest, they know you have your own

Black Mountains.

cooling board

a long-playing poem

I was talking to myself the other night...*to yourself? Do you know how that sounds?* Everybody left me in the studio, gave me some peace, bought a little time to work on what Roberta wanted. *Roberta? What about what you want? How's that for peace?* I forgot how quiet the booth can be when you control the boards, each track an album of its own. *Are you for real? This how you deal with getting pushed around? Stand up, Donny. Backbone son, backbone.* I stood up from the bench for a second...*OK*...looked through the glass...*all right*...saw me looking back, laughed, said Donny, you a sad somebody. *Got that right.* Once I said it, the words wouldn't leave, they just hung around, like songs that are better in your head than on the radio. *What are you saying? What's better than a song on the radio? Can't nobody hear what's in your head?* Exactly.

Process of a Love Song

Saw this sister, lonely,
strolling down 5th.
She had an umbrella,

& there wasn't a cloud
in the sky—bet
she's always dodging clouds.

I'm thinking, she's too pretty
to be alone, & in a second
she wasn't. Some brother

in plaid, a brim as big as mine,
moved up easy, but easy
couldn't hold heat.

They threw words back & forth,
his empty hands & tilted hat
begging "please baby—please."

She backed way,
creased arms carving invisible
dare-you-to-cross boundaries

in the air between them.
She shoved the umbrella
to the center of his chest,

walked away. He didn't dare follow,
didn't look like he could even breathe,
missed a breath or two, heart

stopped with her curse & shove.
He didn't leave that corner
for a good five minutes,

like he thought it wasn't over,
like she would really come back,
have second thoughts

about burying him with the things
he left behind.
I try my best

to blend into sun-scored walls,
to be concrete, chrome—
the panes that mirror

the fracture.
I pass him at the light,
hail a cab back to my apartment,

have a talk with my piano. Ask
if she's ever told any stories
about umbrellas

that are no good for rain.

What Eulaulah Hears (alternate take)

Before I knew his name,

Singing is out, he says.
I loved his song

like raised voices,
hear him sing

if he doesn't let the world.
I can pray all day, but that boy

is crazy, like outgrown clothes
in attics of dust.

I have never met someone
so blessed yet so afraid, too bright

for a back to turn.
It is written in him,

not by or on. Words
are meant to be discarded,

discovered years later
to share the gifts

God gave. So many Sundays
rocking the choir holy

the proof, not the keys.
He gives that freely.

CHEMISTRY

A long time coming, long time—
like dust waiting on rain.
I promise
the only voices I hear, mine
& yours, the music we will make.
It's already written, been in my head
since the day I walked away,
said this partnership was built
on me, not with me. I know
my words are too heavy
to take back, but I've seen the truth
about you & me.

We are a note
one voice can't reach
but two can carry.

CHART POSITION (WHAT HITS & WHAT DOES NOT, TAKE 2)

"Where is the Love" (w/Roberta Flack) 1973 (R&B #1, Pop Top5, Grammy)

"The Closer I Get to You" (w/Roberta Flack) 1978 (R&B #1)

"You Are My Heaven" (w/Roberta Flack) 1980 (R&B #2)*

"Back Together Again" (w/Roberta Flack) 1980 (R&B #2)*

Released posthumously, available on "Roberta Flack Featuring Donny Hathaway."

SESSIONS: NEW YORK (ALTERNATE TAKE)

Who loves me?
Who loves me enough
to lie & say

This is working.

No, don't tell Eulaulah,
Roberta, don't tell
a soul. This
is working.

This is working?

We've got a session tomorrow
at midnight, give me enough
time to decide what's working.

What's working?

What's working?

Yes, what's working—

& where's Roberta?

In her skin—
(undermine).

Exits

My ears are filled with the dead,
voices truer than what speaks today:
suicide melodies, overdose harmonies,

bullet wound improvs.
Robert Johnson was poisoned,
Hendrix, Joplin, Morrison—
all some form of suicide. What if it was me:

the pills, the booze,
the man on a ledge, crowd saying,
Don't do it.

What am I willing
To die for? *What,*
am I willing to die?

cooling board

a long-playing poem

Give me a minute...

...where was I?

101

•

THE OMEGA SESSIONS: EIGHT STEPS CLOSER

Take One
Tell me this:
who is lonely by choice,
wants with no purpose, wishes
to be empty?

Take Two
What's that gotta do with me? Did you see me do it? Then how you know?

Take Three
The book says it's mostly white men,
20-25. Do they think
black men are afraid? Maybe
we've got more to lose.

Take Four
A Rhodes & a Fender is the same thing? Fool, how am I s'posed to know that?

Take Five
I'm doing my best to fill in the blanks.   There's always something missing.

Take Six

That's not what I asked you. You've got a talent for being wrong, you know that?

Take Seven

Tell me,
this who is lonely by choice
wants with no purpose, wishes
to be empty. This is no life
I know.

Take Eight

*First chance, I'm gone. I've had it. No more
playing the corner.*

Tell me

I'm wrong.

MAKE IT ON MY OWN

Number one with a bullet
is waiting, *been waiting. A spot
on the charts with my name,*
my name only.
    Small steps is all it takes,
small steps—that's all.
Come in a fit or a whisper,
at any hour, *doesn't matter,*
long as you get the message,
long as you're up for the game.
    New York is a test—
you know what they say
about making it here—
but I think I get it now,
just needed to say it
out loud, louder
than the voice in my ear.

The Last Supper (Roberta's Apartment, Central Park West)

Roberta played a song today
that I was unprepared for, the unfamiliar

melody my pause once at her table.
From these windows, Manhattan

is the world: blanket of emerald & stone,
a mask for the hazards below.

      No one promised
when we made a way into this world

we would know which day was the last,
be ready when the bed became our cooling board.

I trust the piano, have faith it will take whatever fails
to fall from my mouth & make it clear.

When I get weary, & the notes don't come,
won't come, I testify.   It all becomes song.

Essex House Hotel (alternate take)

There is no note—that is work
& I am weary. Splitting
glass without interruption,

stacking the pieces on my bed,
that is more work than any man
should bear. Had a hard time trying

to break that pain without someone
running to my door, questioning
the commotion. There is nothing now,

this empty room, pages meant for notes
I can't record. No one
to play these blues for. When I land,

oh, the sound:

like wielding John Henry's hammer
as hands, fists that squeeze black red,
pound keys   silent.

cooling board

a long-playing poem

† PERSONNEL

Donny Hathaway: lead vocals, piano, electric piano, organ;

Eulaulah Hathaway: lead vocals on "What Eulaulah Hears" & "In Case You Thought
      It Was Easy"; backing vocals on "Meeting Eulaulah, Howard University,"
      "Negotiating the First Date," "What Stars Are For," "Miss Martha Meets
      Eulaulah," "Whisperers," "An Evening at St. Vincent," "Meds," & "This
      Is Blues";

Drusella Huntley: lead vocals on "Naming" & "Exodus I (Chicago to St. Louis)";

Martha Crumwell: lead vocals on "Ascension (A Lesson for Miss Martha)," "The
      Amazing Donny Pitts & His Magic Ukulele," "Extensions," "The Music:
      An Explanation to Miss Martha," & "Miss Martha Meets Eulaulah";

Roberta Flack: lead vocals on "Roberta, Rebirth," "S.R.O.: Mr. Henry's, Capitol
      Hill," & "Chart Position,"; backing vocals on "Sessions: New York" &
      "The Last Supper";

Curtis Mayfield: lead vocals on "Curtis Breaks It Down";

Jacqueline Bethany: lead vocals on "Midnight Hour"

Phil Upchurch: guitar, lead guitar on "Troubadour, 1971," bass on "Trio";

Mike Howard: lead guitar on "The Bitter End";

Willie Weeks: electric bass;

Earl DeRouen: congas;

Ric Powell: drums;

Fred White: drums on "Troubadour, 1971";

Richard Tee: organ on "Troubadour, 1971";

Hubert Laws: flute;

King Curtis: tenor sax;

Donald Myrick: alto sax;

Marvin Stamm: trumpet;

Morris Ellis: trombone;

Ethel Merkerl: French horn;

Don Butterfield: tuba;

Sanford Allen & Theodore Israel: violin;

Kermit Moore & George Ricci: cello.

Recorded October 1, 1945 – January 13, 1979

BIOGRAPHICAL NOTE

Mitchell L. H. Douglas' poetry has appeared in *Callaloo*, *Crab Orchard Review*, and the anthologies *The Ringing Ear: Black Poets Lean South* (University of Georgia Press), *America! What's My Name?* (Wind Press), and *Zoland Poetry Volume II* (Zoland Books) among others. He was named a finalist for the Stan and Tom Wick Poetry Prize in 2007 and nominated for a Puschart Prize in 2006. A founding member of the Affrilachian Poets, a Cave Canem fellow, and Poetry Editor for *PLUCK!: The Journal of Affrilachian Arts & Culture. Cooling Board: A Long-Playing Poem*, is his debut collection.

Photo credit David Flores

Printed in the USA
CPSIA information can be obtained
at www.ICGtesting.com
JSHW060042150824
68134JS00028B/2601